Abraham Lincoln

A Buddy Book
by
Christy DeVillier

VISIT US AT

www.abdopub.com

Published by ABDO Publishing Company, 4940 Viking Drive, Edina, Minnesota 55435.
Copyright © 2001 by Abdo Consulting Group, Inc. International copyrights reserved in all
countries. No part of this book may be reproduced in any form without written permission
from the publisher.

Printed in the United States.

Edited by: Michael P. Goecke
Contributing Editor: Matt Ray
Image Research: Deborah Coldiron, Susan Will
Graphic Design: Jane Halbert
Cover Photograph: Archive Photos
Interior Photographs/Illustrations: pages 4, 7, 15, 18, 19, 20 & 21 (left): ABDO image
archives; pages 11 & 17: Corbis; pages 21 (right), 22, 23 (right), 26 & 27: courtesy of
Library of Congress, Washington, D.C.; page 23 (left): Deborah Coldiron; page 28:
Eyewire Inc.

Library of Congress Cataloging-in-Publication Data

Devillier, Christy, 1971-
    Abraham Lincoln / Christy Devillier.
       p. cm. — (First biographies)
    Includes index.
    ISBN 1-57765-591-5
     1. Lincoln, Abraham, 1809-1865—Juvenile literature. 2.
    Presidents—United States—Biography—Juvenile literature. [1. Lincoln,
    Abraham, 1809-1865. 2. Presidents.] I. Title.

E457.905 .D48 2001
973.7'092—dc21
[B]

2001022020

Table Of Contents

Why Is He Famous?

Abraham Lincoln

Abraham Lincoln was the 16th President of the United States. He was president from 1861 to 1865. This was during the American Civil War. Many people believe Abraham Lincoln was the best president.

President Lincoln ended slavery. Slaves are people who are forced to work for nothing. These slaves were from Africa. People brought these Africans to the United States. People sold these Africans as slaves. Abraham Lincoln believed slavery was wrong.

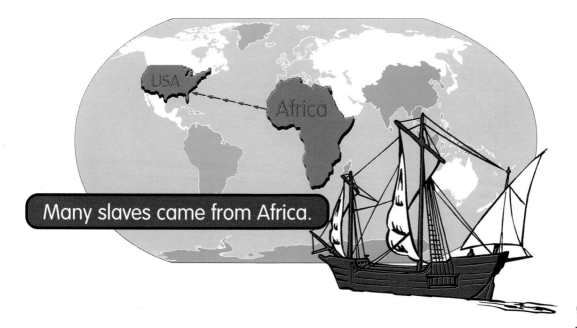

Many slaves came from Africa.

Growing Up

Abraham Lincoln was born on February 12, 1809. He was born in Hardin County, Kentucky. He had one older sister, Sarah.

Abraham Lincoln was born in Kentucky.

Abraham lived in this log cabin.

Abraham's family lived in a log cabin. This log cabin was small. There was only one door and one window. It had a dirt floor.

The United States of America

Indiana

Abraham Lincoln moved to Indiana.

In 1816, Abraham's family moved to Indiana. They did not like Kentucky anymore. Many people in Kentucky owned slaves. Abraham's family thought slavery was bad.

It was hard moving to Indiana. It was on the frontier. They had to build a new cabin. Yet, Indiana was better than Kentucky. Fewer people in Indiana owned slaves. Also, Abraham's family had fewer problems buying land in Indiana.

Reading And Writing

When Abraham was seven, he went to school. He loved to learn. But he could not go to school all the time. His parents needed his help at home.

Young Abraham, or Abe, helped his Dad with the farm. He fetched water. He gathered firewood. Abe chopped wood, too.

Abraham liked to read.

Abe loved to read. It was hard to find books on the frontier. So, he read the same books over and over. He liked Aesop's Fables, Robinson Crusoe, and a book about George Washington. George Washington was the first President of the United States.

Honest Abe

Abraham Lincoln had several jobs. He chopped wood for fences. He worked in a store. He cleared land for settlers.

Abraham worked on a boat, too. He sailed down the Mississippi River. He saw many cities. He sailed all the way down to New Orleans. There, he saw people buying and selling slaves. Abraham felt sorry for these Africans in chains.

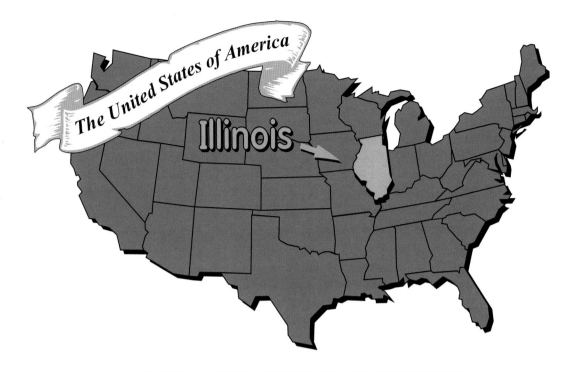

The United States of America

Illinois

Abraham Lincoln moved to Illinois.

Abraham moved to New Salem, Illinois when he was 21. Abraham worked at a store there. He met a lot of people. Everyone liked him. They thought he was honest. He never cheated anyone. Abraham's nickname was "Honest Abe."

Pride For His Country

Abraham loved his country.

Abraham had a lot of ideas. He thought of many ways the United States could be better. He wanted his country to stop slavery. He thought that slavery was unfair.

Abraham was proud of his country. He wanted to see his country do well. So, Abraham decided to be a lawmaker. In 1834, Abraham became a lawmaker for Illinois.

Abraham studied law, too. He became a lawyer in 1837. He had a partner to work with. Abraham's partner was John Stuart. They worked together in Springfield, Illinois.

As a lawyer, Abraham helped many people.

Mary Todd

On November 4, 1842, Abraham Lincoln married Mary Todd. Abraham and Mary had four children.

Mary Todd

Abraham Lincoln with his family.

Mary was from Kentucky. Unlike Abraham, Mary came from a rich family. She knew Abraham was not a rich man. She also knew Abraham was a good and honest man.

The 16th President

On November 6, 1860, Abraham Lincoln became the 16th President of the United States. He was president when many southern states broke away from the U.S. This started the American Civil War.

President Lincoln with Union soldiers in Antietam, Maryland.

Why did the South break away from the United States? The South did not want the U.S. to end slavery. Many farmers in the South used slaves. These slaves worked on farms for free. The South did not think their farms would work without slaves.

President Lincoln working during the American Civil War.

A portrait of a Confederate soldier.

The American Civil War lasted for four years. President Lincoln did not like war. Yet, he did not want the South to leave the U.S. He worked hard to keep the United States together.

President Lincoln with Allan Pinkerton and Major General John A. McClernand in Antietam, Maryland.

On January 1, 1863, President Lincoln signed the Emancipation Proclamation. This very important paper helped to free many slaves.

The Emancipation Proclamation

Many people thought the Emancipation Proclamation was a good idea.

On November 19, 1863, President Lincoln gave a speech. This speech is famous. He gave this speech on a battlefield in Gettysburg, Pennsylvania. President Lincoln's speech is called the Gettysburg Address.

The United States During the Civil War

The states in blue wanted the United States to stay together. They called themselves the Union.

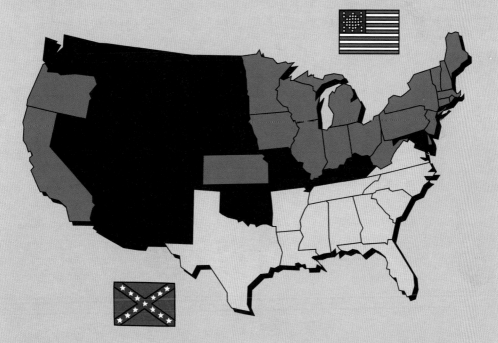

The states in gray wanted to break apart from the U.S. They wanted to form a new country. They called themselves the Confederate States of America.

A Great Man Dies

On April 14, 1865, President Abraham Lincoln was watching a play with his wife. The play was "Our American Cousin." They were watching this play at Ford's Theatre.

Ford's Theatre still stands in Washington, D.C.

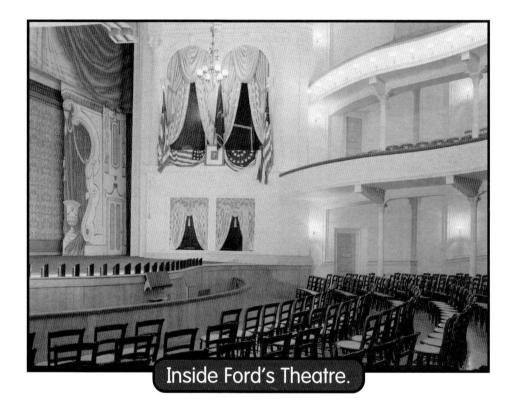

Inside Ford's Theatre.

John Wilkes Booth shot President Lincoln at Ford's Theatre. This great president died. This happened five days after the American Civil War ended.

An American Hero

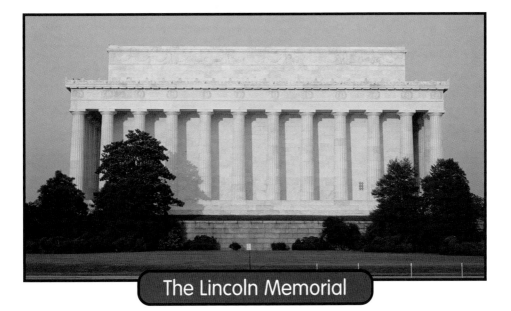

The Lincoln Memorial

Abraham Lincoln is one of the most famous presidents. This great man loved his country. He ended slavery. He helped to end the American Civil War. This American hero worked hard for his country.

Today, people honor Lincoln at the Lincoln Memorial. The Lincoln Memorial is in Washington, D.C. The American people will always remember this great man.

A statue of President Lincoln at the Lincoln Memorial

Important Dates

February 12, 1809 Abraham Lincoln is born in Kentucky.

1816 Abraham's family moves to Indiana.

1828 Abraham sails down to New Orleans on a boat.

1830 Abraham moves to Illinois.

1834 Abraham becomes a lawmaker.

November 4, 1842 Abraham marries Mary Todd.

November 6, 1860 Abraham Lincoln becomes President of the United States.

April 14, 1861 The American Civil War begins.

January 1, 1863 President Lincoln signs the Emancipation Proclamation.

November 19, 1863 President Lincoln gives his famous speech, the Gettysburg Address.

April 9, 1865 The American Civil War ends.

April 14, 1865 John Wilkes Booth shoots President Abraham Lincoln at Ford's Theatre. President Lincoln dies.

Important Words

American Civil War the United States War between the Northern and the Southern states.

Emancipation Proclamation President Lincoln wrote this important paper. It helped to free many slaves.

frontier new land that has very few or no people living on it.

settlers the first people to live on a frontier.

Web Sites

Abraham Lincoln: An Educational Site
http://www.geocities.com/SunsetStrip/Venue/5217/lincoln.html
This site is designed for students and includes "cool" Lincoln facts for kids.

The Life of Abraham Lincoln
http://www.berwickacademy.org/lincoln/lincoln.htm
Published by the students of Berwick Academy, this site features an illustrated timeline of Lincoln's life.

The Time of the Lincolns
http://www.pbs.org/wgbh/amex/lincolns/index.html
This site aptly describes life during the Civil War.

Index